Cosmic Consciousness and Healing with the Quantum Field

-a Guide to Holding Space Facilitating Healing, Attunements, Blessings, and Empowerments for Self and Others

by
Darshan Baba

ॐ

Cosmic Consciousness and Healing with the Quantum Field
By Darshan Baba
Copyright 2016 Darshan Baba

Go to http://siddha-life-mastery.com **now to sign up for a free online course**: Introduction and Experience of Subtle Energy, includes Ancient Secret of the Masters – a Simple Breathing Technique for Increased Awareness, Intelligence, Energy, Health, & Personal Power.

FREE Ebook copy of "A Self Attunement: Maha Moksha Healing" Now available at http://siddha-international.weebly.com Follow the link to get instant access to download!

ॐ

Dedication:
May All Beings Know Peace!

ॐ

A New Beginning

This very moment is blossoming open with the fragrance of sacredness, petals spreading out as Infinite Possibilities, the never ending expression and presence of the One. Here in this sacred moment of Now, within every cell of your Being there is a subtle opening of New Awareness. Feel the breath, feel awareness, and *feel* a simple presence of Being.

This book has brought with it an open portal to the infinity of Being. This "portal" or gateway is completely safe and beneficent, existing as shinning light encodements of the Enlightened Intention of all Masters combined. Receive now the never ending gift of attunement to the all-pervasive Unified Quantum Field of Energy with Unlimited Possibilities; the subtle

ॐ

foundation of all reality giving birth to all that arises within all infinities.

The Masters teaching within all cultures have said that all of creation, mystical knowledge, sciences, and indeed all that is and is not; all of this exists within your own being as inseparable from your own body/mind energy field. Everyone who has attained to Mastery has done so encountering and enkindling with awareness the totality of this mystical knowledge within. Like mirrors reflecting an image back and forth into infinity, the Enlightened Intention of the Masters is in you and you are in them.

This energy of the Enlightened Intention of the Masters enters now into your life as the "Master Healing Ray" with infinite possibilities and no limit to the resources available to serve your growth, healing, well-being, fulfillment and Mastery. Likewise, the energy of this

ॐ

Enlightened Intention of all Masters combined, and the Energy of All that is as Infinite Possibilities accompanies your every step in facilitation of energy work to enkindling the same blessings in others.

This book carries a series of empowerments and a guide to holding space in order to facilitate the energy work you are now being attuned to. This energy work originates from subtle dimensions of being in the form of higher frequencies of energy which exist like a portal to anchor this collective Intention of Mastery, Empowerment, and Illumination from the most subtle and Ultimate dimensions all the way to the grosses realities of Earth. In this way the work seems to do itself from grosser perception, so the greatest way to practice healing work in the Quantum Field is to learn to hold a space of "allow," and increase awareness- pay total attention.

Trust in the all-pervasive and limitless

ॐ

Energy of Infinity which is now directly touching you to bring new awareness and opportunities in life. The thinking mind has all different sets of games it can play with itself as to the perception and nature of self, life, and reality. Allow the mind to set aside these old thinking modes and views, to hold space for this energy to work during sessions with the self and others, and with that space created receive "downloads" or "packages" of energy carrying pure information.

    These high frequency energies packed with information can be in regards to what informs the manifestation of a structure of energy which appears as a physical body composed of its interactions of vibration and particles that assume the form of matter. Or the downloaded energy can be carrying information to re-organize patterns and energy structures of mental perception as well as emotional patterns of

ॐ

reacting, and can also be working to clear up any physical, mental, or emotional toxic build up. The Energy Wave carrying immense amounts of information can be working at incredible speeds on multidimensional levels of being simultaneously, bringing any and all necessary information to inform all areas of the life-energy field to one's highest capacity to accept well-being.

It has been observed by scientists that atomic particles sometimes actually behave instead as a wave carrying information of super-position and multiple possibilities of where and how the particle can be. In the same way these energy waves of information coming from the Infinite Quantum Field can inform the energy field of the recipient and cause a desired total re-organization of the energetic and atomic structures.

Through the energy and awareness of

this quantum field, there truly is no limit to what can be discovered, experienced and achieved. In the way that scientists have prodded at reality in laboratories it has been slow halty progress, but finally after generations of scientists a modern science has brought forth a view of reality that echoes the ancient cosmology of the Vedas.

The benefit of being a conscious and aware being is that this force of Awareness itself can discover and tap into the very fabric of reality because it is Pure Awareness itself. The subtler and smaller physicists break up and experiment with the matter of reality, the more conscious and unified it appears.

You are One with all Infinity, and your awareness is not different from the Unified Awareness of the Zero Point Field/Planck Scale. Magic and miracles can become a reality in everyday life; the reality of everyday life is the miracle of the infinite possibilities of the Quantum Field. The blazing intention of Enlightenment, Empowerment, and Mastery sourced from that frequency of the combined attainment of all Masters, is stronger than any of our doubts, indulgences, or limited modes of thinking. This Pure Awareness with Unlimited power and resources to Being- is Ultimate Reality.

Be open to the Infinite Possibilities of the Universe and willing to experience something brand new but also timeless at this very moment. After you finish reading these chapters take a moment to settle into awareness of the present moment through the breath. Suspend any expectations and increase awareness, and imagine however it might be to your imagination, an all-pervasive Energy Field of Infinite Possibilities.

ॐ

Extraordinary Experience-Practical Guidelines

As you read this book be in a comfortable setting able to rest back and sometimes even lay completely back. When doing this work in person with a facilitator, some of the modalities working with the quantum field start the recipients standing with someone behind them to catch as the wave of energy causes them to enter deeper brain states where the body naturally wants to relax and fall back. For this reason, you should be prepared for the energy received under the guidance of the empowerments from this book to have similar effects on your body in which you may want to completely relax under the influence of new extraordinary experiences.

When you facilitate work with this

energy of infinite possibilities be aware of the effects that this energy can have as well. If you do choose to use the method of "collapsing" as the wave comes in, do have someone to catch behind, watch carefully to ensure they don't fall another direction than you are prepared to catch them, because you will see that the energy waves themselves cause the body to relax into a less than physical state and want to collapse. As the waves of energy containing high frequency information come in, the body may begin to wobble or sway, be ready to improvise and catch them and lay them back on the mat from which ever direction they may go if it isn't back into the arms of the one catching. In this instance if you start to sense in the field that the body may be relaxing away from the catcher, you can use a push of the energy briefly to push them back towards the one catching and the soft mat waiting for them to lie on.

You may also facilitate with someone sitting and able to sit back in a comfortable chair, or from sitting then lay back on the mat (massage table, mattress, bed, a blanket on the Earth etc.) It is often important for the recipient to be able to completely lay back and relax so they can relax into very deep states of being allowing energetic systems and structures to "go off-line" for a period and be completely restructured in a more vital and empowered way. You can also just have people start in a comfortable laying down position, and work from there, that is the recommended method for simplicity.

As the energy waves of "down-loadable" information to re-inform the energy field come in, one may have all sorts of mystical, "kooky", and extraordinary experiences. Recipients often enter into deep meditative states, trances, or other

ॐ

altered states. In "quantum" states of multidimensional experience, one might start speaking in tongues or make other sounds and tones, start moving the body in mudras and postures automatically, have out of body experiences, past life memories, visions of future, etc. There really is no limit when working in the field of Infinite Possibilities. The body may twitch and jerk as changes occur in the nervous system or energy is being released, there may be sensations of energy, vibration, hot and cold, frequencies of sound heard, laughing, crying, shouting, farting, etc.

The body can release energy in many ways and we are carrying diverse patterns of experience in our mind/body energy fields. Be open and free of judgment, holding a space of Love for the profound mystery of being that every bit of this show of reality is.

ॐ

Seemingly strange occurrences are normal under the context of collective and personal evolution of humanity to habitually occupying greater levels of awareness in multidimensional experience. Some people are already strongly receiving the energy of this Awareness Up-leveling without prior knowledge and will be guided to work with you sub consciously by the energy itself. They may have experienced symptoms of the changes occurring such as the body suddenly wanting to collapse and the various signs of high frequency energy working.

Through practice with this energy you will begin to recognize the signs of the energy working by seeing it work with various people, watching the signs and symptoms of this energy effecting deep multidimensional change at high speeds and high frequencies. As well as through having had direct experience with these energies yourself. These symptoms may appear strange to someone undergoing these changes and you can easily help to calm by acknowledging these experiences as merely uncomfortable or new side effects of an overall beneficial process.

The Healing/Guidance Team

You now receive your own team of guides for assisting in working with this Energy of the Quantum Field of Infinite possibilities. This Healing and Guidance Team is also here now in every moment to support you in all aspects of Being, in harmony with the unified whole of Infinity. Whether this "Healing Team" is something that you can now sense or experience in a pragmatic way, to begin just know that you have one.

You can call on this Healing Team at any time you feel in need of assistance, healing or guidance. You will also call on your Healing Team to assist in holding space for others to facilitate working with the energy of infinite possibilities.

Spend some time now centering and becoming fully present through focusing on the breath. Awareness of the breath is a way to calm and center the mind, and what experiences of awareness that arise in the field of mind are intimately connected to the quality of breathing.

As mind calms and settles deeper into the ocean of consciousness away from the surface waves, call upon your Healing Team. Ask for a "download" of energy informing your energy field in a way which helps you to work as a member of this inter-dimensional Healing Team to facilitate the empowering of humanity in a Golden Age of Illumined Knowledge and harmonious existence.

Ask for your Guidance and Healing Team to make their presence known to you through whichever means will work for you personally to have awareness of them. Free of expectations for the experience that may show up and how it should look, simply trust that you have immensely

ॐ

powerful help and support, and also trust that whatever is truly needed will show up when it is needed and when you are ready.

ॐ

Working with Energy

To have a greater pragmatic awareness of energy and the field, the key is to notice subtler dimensions of reality using increased awareness. Like the layers of an onion multiple dimensions of reality are coexisting simultaneously, interwoven as one totality of Being.

On one level the world appears as a world of objects, but in other layers there is seen an ever shinning world. As the sun goes down, this shinning world only appears brighter because the world of objects becomes dark, mysterious, and less defined.

Notice with a given situation or memory there is the dimension of experience that involves thought, while on another level there is feeling and emotions. Another dimension to the experience involves the information coming through the senses such as a physical sensation of the body in seated position. These are all like different layers or dimensions to the same moment in time, coming as information from the Field of Energy that based on your energetic structure of interpretation then carries particular appearances and an experience.

In the same way that you may have been sitting there for a while, and didn't necessarily notice the dimension of the feeling of sitting there or how the body felt in the posture you were sitting until reading called attention to it, so the field of energy may go unnoticed but awareness can shift to bring it to light. To notice the world as energy just start to notice new layers or dimensions to your experience at any given time through increasing awareness. Don't necessarily look for anything in particular, just relax your normal modes of perception and with pure mindfulness be present in the empowered moment of Now, and with this increased Awareness just notice what arises within that field of Awareness.

According to the teachings of the Masters, we select from the infinite possibilities of Pure Energy the world we experience in the same fashion as a dream. The Realized Ones have said that in the same way the mind creates an identity, a body, and a whole world to facilitate dreaming, so too, by the same medium and method does the mind create the same in the supposed "waking" state. The only way that the waking and dreaming state are any different is that they are like different layers or dimensions of the same Being.

Becoming aware in dreaming you might notice that if you gaze at an object too long it starts to shift into something else, and indeed the whole dreaming scene could completely change in an instant. In the waking state something very similar occurs, if you keep the eyes as still as possible while you gaze at an object notice what you experience.

The magic of this past age of humanity is in how they have been able to so consistently and coherently dream this world of separate objects and reason. It takes enormous amounts of energy to create this world and grasp to it as concrete reality out of the many infinities of possibilities that exist as the Unified Field of Ultimate Reality. That is why we must relax our hold on this world and go into sleep or meditation to rest and restore the energy needed to again dream this consistent concrete reality with so many rules and appearances of separateness. Ever notice what happens if you don't sleep or drop into similar brain wave states through meditation? The world will become very dreamlike and rules will seem to bend, it would be hard to experience from a rational and logical dimension for sure.

To practice with dreaming and gain greater control in lucid dreaming, one wants to shift awareness from object to object swiftly and back to a central object as many times as possible to continue the same dreaming scene before it shifts out of control. In this way one can gain greater control of the dreams without them just shifting all over the place out of control. To learn to bend the rules of the waking state and achieve magic the opposite practice of stillness is effective.

Notice how we move from object to object, from thought to thought, activity to activity, constantly doing whatever we can to fill space and create the continuity of our world. Instead create and allow that space, see its presence in every moment, and

ॐ

tapping into a profound stillness within; realize infinite possibilities as a reality.

Gaze at the surface of water, the clear sky, or inside a totally dark room. Without objects to distract the eyes notice what you *see,* in total silence without sounds to distract the ear notice what you *hear.*

Watch the full moon without looking directly at it while keeping the eyes still and notice what you *see.* Look anywhere at anything, then soften focus for a while with the eyes still and pay attention to the field of vision with careful awareness. Notice how in total darkness there is shining light, and in stillness the field of energy is dancing.

Practice rolling the eyes up to look towards the third eye with awareness, while you focus on the breath, and notice what you *see* here. When the eyes are rolled up in this way with relaxed breathing, the brainwaves automatically

ॐ

enter a theta state which is conducive to visionary experience. Concentrate on this point at the third eye to increase capacity for visualization, as well as to increase ability to *see* energy and the subtle dimensions.

When the eyes get comfortable and used to rolling up in focus on the third eye through consistent practice, then start focusing higher to the "Chakra of Knowledge Beyond Words", which is located above the third, and just below the crown. Concentrate here at this chakra as a triangle pointing upwards blazing the brilliant Light of Knowledge beyond words, brighter than ten thousand suns.

Even if you have no sensation or experience of energy and the field at first, *imagine* the energy and play/practice with it. Practice passing it back and forth from each hand, stretch it, cut it, expand and contract energy with the breath. Just experiment with the energy field. Scan the field with Awareness in the hands, moving them slowly around objects and living beings.

Notice the difference between Pushing or Projecting energy and Pulling or Drawing it. Experience how hard it is to Stop all energy flow, and notice the amazing work the intelligent force of energy does when you *Allow* the energy to simply flow.

This Infinite Field of Energy is limitless; the Energy itself of the nature of Unlimited Information and Super Consciousness will be your teacher. Be fully present with Awareness to receive what shows up in the field to serve as a resource to greater levels of Being in peace, fulfillment, and harmony.

Every single witnessed phenomenon is a product of this infinite field of dancing energies. Every moment is teeming with

ॐ

infinite empowered possibilities. Each and every particle is alive with this Super-Conscious all-pervasive field. Anything and everything can reveal profound teachings to one who has awareness, and offers as resource in support of experiencing limitless Being.

As you relax and center through the breath, bring awareness to the Quantum Energy Field of Infinite Possibilities, and call on your Healing/Guidance Team. Calling forth now a "Quantum Download" of energy carrying information specific to this one reading now, in regards to their personal way of becoming aware of and working with energy. Of Infinite Resources and Unlimited Possibilities comes all information, support, and guidance to experiencing and interacting in the world as a Boundless Field of Energy.

Imagine the new rules of the experience available to you as a Being

ॐ

composed of Awareness and Energy with infinite possibilities. Take a moment to pause from reading and *feel* into the now with your breath.

Grounding

When these high frequencies of energy carrying enormous packages of pure information, the content of which is sometimes beyond conceptual constructs of familiarity, come into your field all sorts of experiences may occur. As a result of the energy you may feel very "high", may travel beyond the body, or have an otherworldly experience. In these cases, it is most important to ground. You can ground yourself by imagining sending a cord of light from the crown all the way down into the core of the Earth, thereby integrating the received energies into all dimensions of being here on Earth.

When working with others you should always make sure they are grounded before they part your company. This is to ensure their safety if they go to drive right away or operate heavy machinery or something of the like. This is important because this energy work is very real, it works, and as a result of the energy waves the brain often immediately enters into alpha to theta or even delta brainwave states, which can be synonymous with altered states of consciousness.

To facilitate grounding in another, hold the frequency of grounding yourself as you imagine the white cord going all the way from your crown to the center of the Earth, feeling your feet solidly on the Earth, and imagine the same happening with the one you are facilitating for. You can place a hand on their shoulder, or on their back to transfer physically through touch the energies as you ground.

Holding Frequencies of Energy

All forms of information come in different frequencies of vibration or energy. By learning to identify certain modes of awareness and dimensions of being as frequencies of energy, one can then practice dropping awareness into these particular energetic frequencies. One can then move into these energy frequencies of the various modes of Being with the grace and ease developed by practice in order to hold a space emanating these healing energies.

For example, try this practice of further discovering and holding the frequency of Unconditional Love. This powerful frequency of Unconditional Love is certainly something that is useful to bring to the self, anyone seeking healing, and the world at large.

ॐ

Always bring awareness first to the breath. Through the breath allow awareness to settle into the sacredness and intense presence of Now. Through the breath a connection between worlds and dimensions is interwoven. In the same way breathing can either be a conscious or unconscious process it connects our conscious, sub-conscious, and super conscious mind (the Quantum Field).

There is an immediate shift in awareness facilitated through focusing on the breath resulting in greater Clarity and Presence. Bring that Clarity of Awareness and let it rest in the center of the Heart chakra. Now call forth there in your heart a feeling of Love. Imagine whatever stories, images, or persons that bring a feeling of Love to the Heart. Then as the feeling arises as a tangible experience, single out that *feeling* of Love and imagine it increasing exponentially. Allow all the stories, images, persons, or conditions that helped induce the initial feeling of love fall away, while maintaining the pure *feeling* of the frequency and energy of Love. Continue imagining the Energy of Love increasing in strength of feeling and presence to the greatest intensity that you can comfortably handle at this time.

The more you practice holding and emanating these frequencies the quicker you can access them with greater ease and intensity of potency. In the same way that is described here for practicing the frequency of love one could practice with the energy of Joy, Divine Grace, Forgiveness, Mystery of Being, Infinite Possibilities, etc.

Mind is a mysterious field of magic and mystery. Explore the infinite dimensions of Being. You can ask your Healing Team for guidance, inspiration, and ideas. Just be open to the infinite

ॐ

possibilities with how the magical universe may answer, this guidance often doesn't fit limits of expectation.

All the Resources of Infinity

The portal now opens to the highest dimension of Ultimate Reality, the Field of Pure Energy with infinite possibilities offering never-ending resources of pure power. You can call forth anything from this infinity. You can call in any of the teachers who facilitate and teach this work (found in Bibliography/Resources) as well as tap into the knowledge these energy workers hold. One can call the energetic presence, skill and knowledge of any and all of the Masters of any and all traditions. Through this field of infinite possibilities, the methods and energies of any and all healing modalities are brought forth in the moment, as well as the knowledge and empowerments of each and all mystical traditions and esoteric sciences. This never-ending infinity of the Quantum Field

ॐ

offers the resources and tools as they are needed, freshly in the moment without prior knowledge.

All that has been known, ever will be known, can be known, and more is at your fingertips through the wide open portal to this dimension of the Unified Field-Infinity. Open to receive this never ending gift of Infinity, affirming now that any and all resources, energy, knowledge and empowerments necessary to complete well-being and Mastery will be received automatically and integrated as they are desired or needed to face all that occurs in each moment.

Take time to center awareness through the breath, and then imagine to your greatest capacity of subtle and boundless perception this Quantum Field of infinite resources. Ask for a download coming as a wave of energy to attune you to greater awareness of this Unified Field of

ॐ

Infinity and its presence as resource to every dimension of your life and being. Each time you do this it's like "leveling-up" as you break through old patterns of perceiving, and as they dissolve, more empowering, free, and multi-dimensional ways of Being replace the outdated energy constructs.

The more you practice attuning to this frequency of Infinite Possibilities, the easier it is to simply and naturally move into and be in this Quantum State of Cosmic Consciousness. You can then live in miraculous dimensions of being and hold this space to facilitate in opening a portal to these infinite resources for the attunement and well-being of others.

We are all in this together, and in the Ultimate Reality at the level of the Unified Quantum String Field, we are all One indivisible consciousness. In this way as each of us receives the empowerments of

Infinity the whole of humanity is benefited. It is not really necessary to "do anything" per-say to facilitate energy work, however the story plays out, whichever bodies act to facilitate healing in the Quantum Field, the energy itself does the work.

A few of the newer energy work modalities such as Matrix Energetics simply came to the founders as the energies of the Quantum Field began working in their lives and through them in-order to come into the world and spread to and through others. These modalities were not created here on Earth; they continuously originate and emanate from the higher or subtler dimensions of Pure Awareness and abstract unbound possibilities. In this same way they are coming to you with or without this book, and when you place your hands in the energy field of another with positive intention, then the energy will work for that one's benefit without limit as well.

In order to facilitate the energy work for another when the energy itself causes you to feel drawn to, you want to practice or someone asks you, first of all call on your Healing Team. Then simply move into this same awareness of tapping into the frequencies of the energy field of infinite possibilities you practiced in this chapter, and set the intention that whatever the person you are working with is ready to receive and release at that time will be so with no limits by the power of Infinity. You may want the person either sitting or lying down because otherwise they may "collapse" or fall as the download comes as a wave of energy and they too become temporarily a wave of energy, a little less than physical as the particles open into a wave of other possibilities of being and then collapse back to a new empowered and more harmonious structure of being

ॐ

The Celestial Healer
Archetype of All Healing

Calling on the "Celestial Healer" - archetype and source of all healing modalities, knowledge, and energies. This one comes forth beyond he or she bringing whatever is necessary for the highest healing on all levels that can be received at this time.

As you breathe feel the immensely powerful support and energy of this Being which is the form of all Healing. A deity or manifestation of the One Infinite Energy for the facilitation of all healing ways now joins your Healing Team ready to meet all needs along the path of healing for you and all you meet that can use this one's infinite resources to healing work.

ॐ

ॐ

Hands of the Master

Place your hands on your body (whenever they are free of the book and you are doing these exercises) anywhere it intuits these packages of energy can work or that energy restructuring/support is needed. Remember any time you practice to center in the present moment and increase awareness through the breath. As you place your hands on the surface of the body, pause for a few moments feeling the connection and sensations of energy, and then gently and non-invasive, allow the energetic hands to move past the surface and into the body. With infinite possibilities the hands of energy move to where ever they are needed in the energy field.

Quantum Waves of pure information encoded in energy issue through the energetic hands within the energy-field of the body/mind/emotions, re-informing all structures to more harmonious, fluid, empowered, and free states of Being. Every physical and energetic cell of the body and energy field is illumined with multidimensional Awareness Enlightened with the Intention of all Realized Masters throughout all space and time as One brilliantly shining Light of Knowledge which is Self-Realization.

Through the portal to Infinite Possibilities and the presence of your Healing Team/Guides, the Power and Presence of the Highest Master you conceive of comes into union with your being. Your hands now act as "the Hands of the Master" - emanating That infinite One's power and energy through your hands for blessing, healing, and rekindling Awareness to full Mastery.

As you relax and breathe, feel the

ॐ

Highest Blessings and Energy of the Masters Hands emanating through "your" hands as you touch the body and play in the field in the space around the body. Notice as you move the hands through and sense the energy-field in the space around the body how the energy *feels*, notice different dimensions and layers, as well as other features that can be felt in the energy field.

    As the Energy of the Infinite Quantum Field works through your body, *allow* the Hands of the Masters to work through your hands, so that your hands offer a place-holder for the infinite to work in the lives of others through the sacred medium of touch. These hands while holding space in a person's energy field automatically move to where they are needed. All necessary information shows up in the field the moment it is needed, and the power of infinite resources does not fail to do the work.

Though it should be common sense, here mentioned is some "ethics" in regards to facilitating healing with touch. In facilitating holding space for healing work and spiritual attunements, one should of course respect social and personal boundaries, and not touch the recipient in ways that would cross those boundaries.

The Ascended Master-Self Integration Point

Center and relax into the profound moment of Now through the breath, and allow your awareness to heighten. High above the crown of the head sits your Ascended Master Self, blazing brilliant Light of Self-Illumination and Self-Realization. Imagine yourself sitting there like a deity in Ultimate Realization of Mastery, in a space beyond the lifetimes past, present and future, but in full Awareness of the Entire Life-Stream, and how each and every moment fits together as One Integrated Indivisible Light of Knowledge and Realization.

Raise your hand, similar to how you would to get a teacher's attention for an answer to a question, and call with mental energy of intention upon this Integration

ॐ

point of your Ascended Master Self. Connect this moment of Now to that Integrated Wholeness and Perfection, feel the strength and wholeness of this One indivisible life-stream and Being of Perfect Mastery. "You" maybe are not who the mind thought "you" were, compared to the Infinite Power, Wisdom, and vast nature of your True Being; the stories and clusters of thought of this small lifetime that were identified as "you" are fleeting and small.

Feel from your upraised hand an antenna like a laser of energy connects with your Mastered Self, and with firm determination to have Clarity of Being bring forth a download. *Allow* your smaller self to surrender its relative nature if only momentarily to receive the Highest Blessings of your Ascended Master Self which pertain to this incarnation, this moment: Now.

Facilitating for others this hand raising

technique is a powerful tool. You can place one hand on the person you are working with, and raise the other asking for assistance from your Healing Team, or the councils of Masters and Light beings that guide the beings of Earth. One can raise the hand calling silently on the field of Infinity, or calling on the "Ascended Master Self Integration Point" of the recipient. First connect to and hold the frequency of your own Ascended Master Self, then visualize the person with you as their Ascended Master Self high above the crown. Perhaps you see them seated on a lotus, deity like and radiating in that eternal timeless moment of the entire life-stream's integration in One Perfected Being of total Mastery. Connecting the person in this now to that Perfection, ask their Master Self that they may receive whatever is helpful from that Integration Point in this now, and any blessings from that omnipotent and all-knowing Self that may be of assistance to their lives now.

It seems like the simplicity of holding the space for infinite possibilities to occur is powerful and profound enough. However, for whatever reason it may be, this body now writing has seen profound shifts occur in a recipient's field through connecting to this "Ascended Master Self Integration Point." The effects of this tool are not so subtle that often they can be seen instantaneously and physically. For example, the facial expression, and whole body immediately relaxing as the person drops into a deeper state of altered consciousness. In the personal practice of the author, meditating with this Integration point of Self Mastery has been profoundly helpful and empowering.

The Fountain of Youth- Life Force Energy

From the dimension of Pure Energy of the nature of unlimited possibilities, comes a never ending resource of Life-Force Energy. This energy comes to you as a gentle stream, and then when you are ready as a flood like a down pouring waterfall, washing through your entire energy field. Allow yourself to relax into the moment filled with life force energy through the breath. This download of life force energy comes shinning like billions of tiny suns entering each and every cell, all systems and structures of the body are enlivened with never ending vitality of life force and energy.

The appearance of a physical body manifests by the power of the infinite quantum field. *Allow* the infinite energy of this field to enliven every bit of the body with Primordial Energy and Pure Awareness. Be willing to let go of stagnant programs of energy that are not conducive to health without limits.

There are numerous people in history who have lived hundreds of years long. There are also stories and evidence of people who achieved Mastery to the level that the body turned to pure light as all aspects of Being were enflamed with the limitless energy and Pure Awareness of Infinity.

Allow yourself to be open to this possibility of Immortal Health and Well-Being, receive the gift of a never ending well spring of life force energy. If the mind has resistance or doubt to accepting this possibility of limitless health, ask yourself to at least be open to the possibility. It is very unlikely that a given experience can be had unless it is first open as a possibility.

ॐ

Tap into and hold this frequency of "the Cosmic Fountain of Youth"-source of all life force energy, for all types of healing for self and others. Just be free of expectations to the outcome.

What occurs each time with any given session is a unique experience free of how it might be expected. All sorts of factors contribute to the show arising in the infinite quantum field at every given moment. Anything is possible without a boundary, as any given person continues to draw certain patterns of experience out of the infinite possibilities that exist, the wise would have to stop and ask themselves why. What you truly believe is possible will to a large extent set the boundary of your experience.

Practice allowing boundaries of mind such as thinking you "know" this world to relax, and open to the infinite. Consistent practice with these exercises will ensure

ॐ

amazing new experiences of Cosmic Consciousness.

Facilitating

Facilitating this work is so simple the rational mind could almost dismiss it looking for something else dressed up more complicated and embellished. But this method is profoundly powerful, the Energy of Infinite Possibilities has no limit, there is no method or teaching that it cannot absorb or provide.

Through this book as a place holder you have been attuned by the Energy of Infinity itself, merely by having been attuned to this Energy, whenever you place your hands in another's field this energy is pretty much guaranteed to work. In the beginning both you and the receiver may just be surprised at how real, obvious, and un-subtle the effects can be at times. At others the effects may be so subtle as to bypass attention; the Energy of the

ॐ

Quantum Field is still working. As long as the facilitator and/or receiver don't have any weird underlying intention that would block the flow of energy, *something* is happening. Just trust in the power of One Unbroken Infinite.

To give the rational mind something to work with, we will give a basic structure of how a session could be facilitated.

- First always start by bringing awareness to the breath.
- Call in and connect to your Healing Team/Guides, as well as the Support Team of the receiver.
- Imagine a portal opening, and connect with the Dimension of an Energy Field of Infinite Possibilities and Resources.
- Continue to center Awareness with the Breath.
- Pay total attention to the moment, Increase Awareness.

- Through this enhanced awareness be ready to listen to whatever intuitive guidance and *feelings* arise as to where to move the hands, as to what to say, and when to remain silent.
- As a general rule of thumb as to where to start if there's no other momentary guidance, you can place one hand cradling gently at the back of the head in the occipital region, and the other hand gently on the forehead (or simply hovering near the body without touching). Or if they are lying down on their backs, with a hand over the heart.
- After the energy has clearly started working, and they are in an altered state, don't talk at that point unless you receive clear strong guidance otherwise. You will notice when you start having these extraordinary multi-dimensional experiences that

ॐ

talking only relates to certain dimensions and then distracts from others.

⚜ If they are seemingly having trouble entering a "Quantum State", the right type of talking and language will help them to access it. It is useful to have a general understanding of Hypnosis for this purpose. You can help by bringing the subconscious mind into play by having them imagine perhaps "Infinite Possibilities", or what it would feel like if this Quantum Energy was working just how they desired.

⚜ As they enter into the "Quantum State" and the energies are working, continue to remain centered and alert with the Breath.

⚜ Hold a Space of *Allow* throughout, because in this state of allow the energy can do anything.

⚜ Allow the energy-field and all the

ॐ

information of the present moment to guide where to move your hands during the session to continue facilitating the movements of energy.

⚚ If the hands aren't drawn to move to anywhere else simply sit back and hold a space of allow, in Awareness of Infinite Possibilities.

⚚ When you feel complete and the recipient is still off in an altered state, continue to hold a space of Infinite Possibilities and sit quietly.

⚚ If they remain "out" for an extended period of time and you are able to leave them alone (such as they are a family or friend at your/there house, or you are working with a group and can come back to them later, etc.) then do so and allow them to come back when ready.

⚚ If you are unable to let them remain deep in the state due to time or another issue, call them back by holding their feet and then gently talking to them, or with a touch on the shoulder.

⚜ After the Session is the complete the energy continues to work whenever the person's energy field is in a conducive state, and the immense packages of gifts received often unravel themselves over time.

⚜ Make sure they are "Grounded" before driving or interacting with dangerous machinery or any other such tasks of the modern world.

Don't make any promises. By the power of infinite possibilities healing can and does occur, and how that healing shows up and how it occurs has no limits.

Allot of factors play into when and how healing occurs in an individual's life. Healing with the Quantum Field is limitless and includes energy working at speeds and levels that could be considered "miraculous healing." Some people are not immediately convinced or open to the possibility of such instantaneous healing, and need repetition or some props to convince them.

In some cases, the symptoms of dis-ease are actually the catalysts in a person's life which are guiding and driving them to true Holistic Healing on levels beyond easing surface symptoms. In such a case the symptoms or condition will persist until the person is guided through all the means necessary to facilitate the deep Holistic Healing that is being sought from a level beyond the conscious mind which is vastly more powerful in influence. After undergoing a profound shift and change of their entire life, re-orientated in a more empowered way, someone with a dis-ease noticing how the presence of the event in life has led them to greater over all empowerment will feel grateful in spite of the "challenge" they faced and even *because* of it. At this point the symptoms are no longer needed and they often disappear, leaving the person healed of the original condition they thought they were seeking to heal, and empowered to even greater Holistic Health.

This is why according to the method transferred by this book, we don't make promises, or even aim energy at someone's symptoms they may have said they came to you for. Instead of feeding energy to the apparent cause of dis-ease, we just hold the space of the Energy of Infinite Possibilities, in overall support of Wholeness and wellness of Being, and absolutely anything can occur in that "quantum" space.

In that space with the Energy of Infinite Possibilities working we could not

ॐ

even comprehend a limit to the experience available. Thus it's hard to say to someone what will happen or what they can expect.

Each sacred moment of this Quantum Connection to Infinity is something brand new and eternal. When the "individual" field is renewed and rekindled with Life Energy through re-connecting to the Energy Field of the Infinite, that "individual" field pulls out something unique from infinity.

Another thing to be aware of is that as long as the medical system is corrupted for profit, then you are not (legally) allowed to say that you have any authority to diagnose, treat, or cure any disease. If information comes to you in regards to diagnosis, you will have to be very careful what you do with information if you have any concern with the law. Also one should be aware that sometimes this information may not be helpful to healing.

Perhaps your only concern and focus

ॐ

is in the greater empowerment of an Ultimate Reality of Infinite Possibilities, then you probably rarely have concerns on your mind and if so only superficially, because your mind probably usually occupies a space of infinite possibilities and support in everything.

By making Awareness of the Quantum Field of Infinite Possibilities a lifestyle, all of one's Being becomes a force of emanating that never-ending resource of blessings and healing. Through consistent practice the ability to hold these frequencies and transmit them becomes sharpened, clarified, and intensified.

Every time you bathe and drink, call in the energies of Infinite Possibilities to bless the water. Also practice with water and notice the energetic qualities of water. Water has a quality of storing information in the same way things dissolve in it; you can utilize this quality of water to raise it to

ॐ

incredibly high frequencies. Perhaps water then is one of the most powerful medicines on Earth when combined with these celestial frequencies.

Before you eat charge the food with these energies of Infinity, this can even change the molecular structure of the food to enhance its value to the body. When you go to sit in a seat after someone, beforehand you can clear and charge the chair with high frequency energies. You can leave a program of healing and blessing energy for everyone who ever sits there afterwards.

When you feel tension in a room bring in energies to clear, harmonize, and create a peaceful feeling. You can download a "Fountain of Youth" program for your elder's (or your own) shoes, walker or cane, etc.

Practice with pets, plants, rocks, whatever your life offers that's *your* playing

ॐ

field. Be creative, through practice and playing with energy in the field of energy, they become a pragmatic affair.

The One Heart Attunement

In this sacred moment of Now, by the Power of All the Masters Combined, the Energy Field of Infinite Potential, and the Power of Pure Primordial Love, receive the Attunement of "The One Heart". As you relax into the breath with increased awareness, your heart merges with the Primordial Archetype of One Indivisible Heart of Pure All-Pervasive Awareness, emanating the original un-contrived Pure Love of All. Your Heart is completely purified in this archetypical blueprint of the sacred heart chakra, and emanates in union with this Unconditional-Love pervading all Infinity as the Self in the Heart of All Beings.

This perfection of the Sacred One Heart and the Eternal Song of Love en-flames within your heart as clear wisdom of unity and the indivisible strength of One.

ॐ

Imagine that there within the heart a "Three-Fold Flame" appears, spinning pink, blue, and golden light; the Flame of the I Am Divine Presence. The pink represents the Unconditional Love of One Heart, the bluish white flame is the Divine Will, and the golden light flame represents Divine Knowledge and Awareness. The three-fold flame swirls from now through every moment of the Eternal Now, always with you bringing forth the qualities and gifts of Divine Awareness, while dispelling through the Light of Knowledge all appearance of lack and limitation. This three-fold flame burns through all obstacles and brings to realization in ultimate clarity: Perfection and Mastery.

The all-pervasive energy- Infinity itself ensures and empowers these attunements. This limitless Pure Awareness of the One guides each one to receive their own expression and blessings of the Infinite.

ॐ

These light codes of Empowerment shine brighter than the sun.

ॐ

ॐ

White Light Transmutation

Relax and center with the breath as you open to receive a package bringing you a method to transmute any and all lower or "negative" frequencies of energy such as worry within or aggression without. There are infinite ways to transmute energy, with any apparent problem there are many solutions.

This book gives the "White Light Transmutation" empowerment, however you can ask the field of infinity for anything. As the portal opens to Pure Primordial Power - Energy of Infinity, into your energy field floods pure high intensity White Light. This white light is so intensely bright that it would block out all other sights by blinding with the intensity of its brightness. This energy of white light burning any malevolent or lower frequencies with intensity "hotter than fire" enters each and every cell of your body and energy field. As this white light fills your field clearing negativity and promoting empowerment, it is stored in your energy field as a program of protection.

This "White Light Transmutation" program is always within your energy field, activating instantly to transmute any lower frequency energy brought near your field. This white light also surrounds your energy field as a protective light so that everything attracted to your life is in harmony with higher dimensions of being in the world. The white light clears your way for healing and mastery, with protection in a field of interacting energies.

Energy Frequency of Moksha

The energy frequency of Moksha is a state of Pure Awareness which is the subtlest knowledge beyond division of words or clusters of concept, thought, and reason. Moksha is the supreme Light of Knowledge which illuminates the infinite possibilities as One Indivisible Unity beyond opposites and extremes such as unity or duality. Do not try to conceptualize or understand the liberation or Ultimate Freedom of Moksha.

As you relax and center through the breath, the energies flow through the open "gateway" from all Infinity in Super Potent form. The download of the program carrying attunement to and the experience of the "Frequency of the Energy of Moksha" comes to bring the Wish Fulfilling Gem of Moksha to full Awareness in this

ॐ

one reading now. This Energy of Moksha also reaches out to touch the field of any and all others who come into contact with you who are also so fortunate as to be willing to receive the Blessing and Supreme Empowerment of Ultimate Freedom-Moksha.

Because this Ultimate Freedom of Moksha defies conception and thought, try chanting this ancient Sanskrit: Moksha. Repeat this silently or aloud to connect with the Energy of Moksha, while you just let go and *allow* yourself to *just be.*

Receive the gift of Crystal Clear Illumined Awareness shinning as the light of Ultimate Freedom. May this frequency of energy bless anyone and everyone you meet who so desires with the same Light of Moksha.

Bring all attention fully to the present, settle into the breath, and just practice Pure Awareness. Pure Awareness is the

ॐ

nature of Moksha; spontaneous enjoyment of Awareness in boundless and infinite Freedom.

ॐ

The Central Axis of Being

Running from the core of the Earth and ascending above the crown into the cosmos is the "Central Axis of Being", which acts as the line of incarnation and exit from this world. All the other dimensions of Being within this world move around and are moved by this deep inner dimension of Being. This "line" stores purpose and intention for this particular incarnation and is therefore a very useful tool for helping self and others to re-discover a feeling of purpose and synchronicity in life.

This deep inner dimension of the central axis of Being is also a priceless resource of Being. Through centering awareness and mastering movements of energy and intention within this subtle energy channel (called the sushumna in Sanskrit), the Yogis achieve mastery over

ॐ

matter. Through this subtle dimension one can also attain to Profound Transcendental, mystical, and all-comprehending states of consciousness.

As you relax and center through the breath, *allow* awareness to settle towards this "Central Axis of Being." As the wave of Energy carrying Quantum Possibilities and liquid light information pours through the central channel it clears a straight path from the "Ascended Master Self Integration Point" to the root chakra at the perineum. The energy then rises gently, as you imagine a downwards pointing triangle blazing with light moving upwards along the spine to meet the triangle pointed upwards at the secret "Chakra of Knowledge Beyond Words," located just above the third eye and below the crown. Imagine these two triangles join at the secret chakra forming a six pointed star (like the Star of David) filling the mind with

ॐ

a dazzling Light of the union of Pure Awareness and Infinite Energy. From the ecstatic bliss of Union, nectar like substance drips from the "Soma Chakra" located just below the secret chakra, and nurtures every aspect of Being with Divine Nature.

Bring Awareness deeply into "the central axis of Being," now shinning brilliantly within, alight with the energies of empowerment through the Quantum Field. Feel a spontaneous deep sense of purpose, and trust that the Universe as an Infinite Super Conscious Being- all that you see, will simply manifest synchronicities re-enforcing your purpose. This Infinite Conscious Field is ever in support of your work and play on Earth, now providing all the tools and props for this game of life with miraculous powers of synchronistic manifestation.

Hold this frequency of "the Central

Axis of Being", the deep inner dimension of incarnation and intention, to help facilitate this alignment when someone seeks to connect to a sense of purpose, as well as for deep Knowledge of Inner Being. This Energy Frequency is also very good to practice for all the various benefits of entering deep into Awareness of the Field.

This central energy channel being the point of incarnation and exit is a good space to hold for those who are "dying." Drop into this Frequency of the central axis of Being, and then raise your Awareness to connect with your "Ascended Master Self Integration Point", as you hold a space of Infinite Possibilities for the departing or already deceased, connect them with their own "Ascended Master Self Integration Point" and simply *allow*. The departing will be helped through this pathway to the highest and most free state that they can attain.

Chakras

You are probably familiar with the standard system of seven chakras; if not you can look into it to give the rational mind something about where they are etc. Whatever you think you may know about the chakras, the way to truly know them is to directly experience them.

Each chakra is a whole sphere or dimension of Being. Bring Awareness with the breath to each of these centers and rest there for some time to experience that chakras particular dimension of Being. There are also good CD's such as Jonathan Goldman's "Chakra Chants" which are carefully designed to the frequency of each chakra, and are a valuable resource for attuning to and practicing the chakra frequencies.

As you relax and center through the breath, call forth your Healing/Guidance Team, and bring Awareness to the Field of Infinite Possibilities. In the form of a wave of light encodements carrying information as energy, comes a program for clearing, aligning, balancing, and healing chakras.

Take further time to relax, breath, and *allow*, as these energies flow and integrate into your energy field. As this energy integrates, the information is stored so that any time your field interacts with another's for blessing and healing the frequencies are easily and automatically accessed as needed.

As you rest for a moment, stay centered in the present moment of now, through the breath. The Ocean of Infinite Possibilities is washing over you now, be sure that you are present for all the

ॐ

Blessings that Infinity has to offer here Now, *this moment.* Crystal Clear, Purity of Awareness... shine forward in all your Glory, Intensity and Power in the ever present reality of... Now!

ॐ

Archetypes

Archetypes are powerful resources for living life and tools for healing. One could download a program of the archetypical blueprint of the healthy human body, or the blueprint of the perfectly healthy archetype of a particular chakra.

One can call from the never-ending resources of the Infinite Quantum Field the archetype of the father or the mother, the wife or the husband, the archetype of the romantic lover, the leader, you get the idea. Not to try to fit our own or another's expectations or molds, but simply to tap into the never-ending resources available to use what works for you to create greater ease of Being, practicality, and magic in your life.

Discover different archetypes in the

ॐ

world and the field that work for you. Maybe the Tao, or the Earth, maybe the Central Galactic Sun or the center of the Universe. Why not just experiment and play in the realms of Infinity?

One can also download packages carrying immense amounts of information from a parallel reality existing in infinite possibilities where the desired objective is already attained and all related knowledge is already skillfully known. As this information in energy integrates into the field of mind whether it is consciously or sub-consciously received the information is present in the field and you will see it affect differences in *this* world

All this information is already an intimate part of our Being in the Super Conscious Mind. What limits could there possibly be to the Super Conscious Unified Quantum String Field of Infinite Possibilities? The only limits are

ॐ

determined by doubt and belief, by dream or by Pure Awareness.

ॐ

The Field of Mind

Tend to the Field of Mind and with mindfulness pay attention to what you seed, feed, and allow to grow there. By now it should be clear that the nature of mind and the Self are something vast, and what is thought is not always true, or its truth may hold little empowering value.

Thoughts are a product of mind, you are not your thoughts, and yet the modes of thought and perceptions of mind seem to color the experience of reality. Hmm... In that case one should indeed be very careful with their thoughts if these thoughts have *so much* influence on how reality is experienced. Just this space in realizing that you are not your thoughts and that those thoughts may not be true, creates profound freedom to act instead of react.

ॐ

With mindfulness pay attention to what you have in your mind. By dis-identifying with these thought forms that no longer serve you, they are no longer fed and no longer grow.

The reality is the Infinite Field which mind arises in itself, teeming with all possibilities; the images there contained within are a constantly changing show. With this Knowledge let your garden in the field of mind be fruitful with those ways of being and perceiving in the world that Empower and bring you Freedom as well as Harmony with all Creation.

With the image of the mind interfacing with the Infinite Quantum Field of Energy like a P.C. with the internet, it's easy to *see* the infinite possibilities that mind has access to. Through cultivating Awareness and Mindfulness, mind becomes a profoundly powerful tool, no longer the realm of experiencing confusion and suffering through repeating old patterns of thought and action. The field of mind becomes a playground to infinite new ways of being and experiencing the Self in the new more expansive and only rule of the Sacred Awareness of Infinity, a simple wholeness.

Cultivate the field of mind, and don't just let it run a-muck with anything growing there. In this way gain powerful freedom in the active participation of your life in the field of infinity. A carefully tended field of mind emanating its own spontaneous Joy and Peace arising from the nature of Pure Awareness, thereby just dancing with the Infinite Limitless Energy, such a mind naturally emanates inspiring, harmonizing, blessing, and healing energies to the surroundings through the Unity of the Quantum Field.

ॐ

ॐ

Affirmations as Tools to Facilitate

These affirmations can be used as tools to call in the energies in order to facilitate the work for yourself and others. They are not necessary but may be helpful as a tool so that the rational mind feels as if it is doing something to facilitate energy work. As has been mentioned, the energy of infinite possibilities itself will guide you and seem to facilitate the work itself.

- I call upon the presence of my Healing Team and Guides
- I call upon the Celestial Healer source of all Healing Knowledge and Energies
- A portal now opens to the Dimension of a Field of Infinite Possibilities
- A wave of Pure Energy comes to support this one to receive all the Blessings and Healing that are ready

ॐ

to be received, and to release those patterns of energy that are ready to be released at this time.
- I call Upon the Energy of Infinite Possibilities
- I call upon the Energy of Moksha
- I call upon the Ascended Master Self Integration Point
- I call forth the energy of any plant medicines, gems/minerals, or Mantras that may be of use for healing in this moment of now.
- I relax and *allow*, holding a space of/for Infinite Possibilities.
- All of this is arising from a Unified Quantum Field; the only thing that's real is Infinite Possibilities...
- I AM Infinite Possibilities...
- There is no past, there is no future, there is only Infinite Possibilities!

12 Strands of DNA Activation

Be prepared to completely lay back and relax undisturbed for a period of time. Breathe in, and as you let the energy out release old programs involving energetic density.

Relax as you center through the breath and become aware of Infinite Possibilities. A portal now opens to Awareness of the very fabric of reality - an Infinite Unified Quantum Energy Field with no limit to the possibilities this Pure form of Power can manifest. Open yourself in a state of *allow* to receive the Gift of a download of energy carrying all the information necessary to facilitate "The 12 Strands of DNA Activation".

From the Field of Infinity comes this wave of energy filled with shining light encodements, dazzling in their brilliance.

ॐ

These Light Codes enter each and every cell of your body whirling, spinning, and weaving with Light the DNA Helix into twelve strands, integrating twelve dimensions of Being into One multi-dimensional Light body with limitless potential.

Relax into Sharpened Awareness with full presence of the Now through the breath, and allow yourself to lie back as your system and energetic structures are reconfigured to integrate this energy-information. Just be with the breath and trust in the Power of Unified Infinity and your Healing Team/Guides to facilitate the up-leveling of your DNA.

This "12 Stranded DNA Activation Program" integrates into your energy field and continues to work in a safe way until your desired level of multi-dimensional experience is achieved. This "12 Stranded DNA Activation Program" also initiates at any time your energy field is in facilitation of energy work and the recipient's field is ready and able to incorporate this blessing as a useful resource.

The solfeggio frequency 528hz has been proven to facilitate miraculous healing, including restructuring of the DNA. Obtaining a CD or tuning forks tuned to solfeggio frequencies, or going on the internet, you can hear the solfeggio frequency of 528hz to attune yourself to and practice dropping into this space for facilitating healing and for quickening or re-enforcing the DNA empowerments in yourself and others.

ॐ

ॐ

Ascension Attunements

To follow is a series of attunements that can lead to "Ascension" through full activation and achievement of "the Rainbow Body" or Immortal Light Body. The energy work of the Quantum Field of Infinite Possibilities is ascension facilitating work, helping everyone encountering this amazing work (not by chance) ascend levels to greater fulfillment and well-being in a practical way according to each one's own desire and pathway. Through this energy of Infinite Possibilities helping us to up-level and ascend to higher dimensions of life, the complete transfiguration of the "physical" body to pure light can be achieved by those who are so inclined.

Please pace yourself with the "downloads" offered here, these are big packages carrying immense amounts of information. Moving too fast could simply produce some perhaps undesired but beneficial side effects such as but not limited to physical detox symptoms, emotional detox, or need of extra sleep. Rapid life changes could occur just as fast as you move into the field.

These positive benefits will occur anyways but at a pace that is never more than your Guides and Healing Team know you can handle. If you are moving ahead with intensity and eagerness to absorb as many of these huge downloads as fast as you can, then you are asking for it. If you do ask for it just be sure you are ready.

It's also very good practice to repeat all the various attunements, exercises, and empowerments in this book multiple times. Even if you had a *profound* experience the first time with every one of them, they will only get better. Practice will help you to really anchor the awareness of the

ॐ

Quantum Field in yourself and your-(Supreme) Self in the quantum field.

ॐ

ॐ

Light of Supreme Grace

As you relax into full Awareness of the present empowered moment of now in the breath, call in the support of your Healing Team. Imagine the portal to the field of Infinite Awareness energy opening.

With immense Love and Gratitude to the Infinite, receive the gift of a Supreme Empowerment Here and Now. The wave carrying your personal attunement to "the Light of Supreme Grace" now fills every cell of your body and energy field with this Immortal Nectar causing all aspects of your Being to shine with the Supreme Light of Divine Grace.

Breathe into the here and now, into *this* powerful moment of the profound. Enter into and hold a space of allowing Infinite Possibilities as you have been practicing. "Supreme Grace Light, Supreme

ॐ

Grace Light, Supreme Grace Light, come and fill us with the Supreme Light of Grace... Supreme Grace Light, Supreme Grace Light, Supreme Grace Light come fill us with the secret to where you originate... Supreme Grace Light, Supreme Grace Light, Supreme Grace Light come activate our Ascension Flight..."

This Light of the Supreme Grace of Super Conscious Infinity carries all the knowledge which can even literally grant physical immortality. If you truly surrender all limiting programming to this Light of the Supreme Grace, in the all-pervasive Unconditional Love which is a product of Unified Awareness, then your body *will* begin to grow younger converting into a body composed of Pure Light impervious to disease, environment, or harm.

The gifts of the Ultimate Reality-Infinite Possibilities, and the Past Masters providing these downloads, have come to give you Knowledge concerning the true boundaries to your experience, it will be up to you and your Intent to be able to meet them in total receptivity to these overflowing blessings.

Allow any structures and programs promoting density and limitation to be released. Be open to the infinite-possibilities of the Universe, and the immense gifts offered by this Spontaneous Mystery of Being.

The fabric of reality, an all-pervasive field of energy with infinite abilities, is the essence composing your Being. This all-pervasive One is naturally filled with the Self beneficent quality of Supreme Love. The "Supreme Grace Light" is the manifestation of this Supreme good intention and Love. By this force of the Light of Grace the Knowledge of Perfection and Mastery comes with ease.

The body can be turned to light in this

ॐ

way, as long as doubts are removed and one is beneficent to all. This program and Blessing is under the guidance and inspiration of Siddha Rama Linga Swami, who first went backwards in age, then turned His body to Light and disappeared. Rama Linga Swami's favorite Name to sing to and call the Divine by was "Arul Perun Jyoti- Supreme Grace Light." That's how Rama Linga Siddhar turned his body to Immortal Light, simply singing to the Supreme Light of Grace with Love...

"Supreme Grace Light, Supreme Grace Light, Supreme Grace Light, oh how you fill my cells with sacred Bliss!"

Expanding Space Filling with Light

Connect now with your Healing Team and the Field of Infinite Possibilities through the breath. Let awareness expand and increase with each breath, as you relax and let go deeper into the sacred presence with each exhale. As you continue to breath, you continue to relax, and your awareness continues to expand with shinning increase.

Begin to breathe into the space within the mind/body field. Feel awareness in the space within the cells, between the molecules, space in between the atoms, space within the nucleus of the atom, and ongoing into infinity opening into greater and greater expanses of space. Breathe deeply into those spaces, as you breathe out letting go of energies that may have been stuck in any of the spaces. Feel with each inhale the space expanding, and as it expands it holds greater capacity allowing for it to fill now with more and more High Frequency Light. As you exhale release all unconsciousness, heavier energies, and limiting programming or belief systems. Continue to practice breathing in this manner for a while seeing your energy grow brighter and more expansive.

Solfeggio Frequencies

Bring full Awareness to the Infinite Magic and Possibilities of the Sacred Moment of Now. Connect to All Dimensions of Being with the breath, as the portal opens allowing the inflow of Primordial Power-the Energy of Infinity.

Open and *allow* yourself to receive a package of energy carrying empowerment of the Solfeggio Frequencies. The information carried as the Solfeggio Frequencies integrates into your energy field for the purpose of activating as an automatic tool to facilitate healing and ascension empowerments for self and others.

Continue to allow yourself to relax and connect to the Infinity of your Being in awareness of the breath bestowing the miraculous fit of the present. Close your eyes for a few minutes, and let everything just take a few moments of pause and rest. Imagine what it would be like to be a Master of the Quantum Field.

The solfeggio frequencies have been scientifically proven for vast healing and empowering benefits. They represent an ancient harmonic scale that was apparently lost to a majority of humanity until re-discovery. Listening to these Solfeggio Frequency tones can be immensely supportive of the work in the Quantum Field, and act as a quickening agent to total multi-dimensional Awareness.

These Solfeggio's are good frequencies to practice holding, the practice integrates these downloads to greater practicality. The Solfeggio Frequencies have now been subconsciously integrated into your energy field, and will automatically arise whenever they are useful for facilitating healing.

ॐ

The Dharma Sangha Attunement

This is a download through the Quantum Field to attune you to the Community-Sangha of all Sacred Traditions-Dharma. This "Dharma Sangha" includes all deities, realized Masters and Teachers, all those Illumined One's sacred knowledge, and all the forms of God/Goddess of all traditions. This "Dharma Sangha" exists as an actual community like unity among the Great Entities of all Sacred Traditions existing in the subtle realms, and working together with this force of Unity to achieve the same on Earth in the ushering in of the Golden Age.

Attuning to this council or sangha your energy field will have access to the Teachings, Support, and Wisdom of all Sacred Traditions and their Teachers-

ॐ

Deities. When you hold space for another any Teaching or Master from this Sangha of all will readily and easily come to support through this link in your energy, with who and what being specific to any of the infinite possibilities of diversity of people you may serve in this way.

Center and relax into this Infinite moment of now as you breathe, call the support of your Healing Team, and bring Awareness to the Quantum field of Infinite Possibility. As you breathe you relax even more naturally and at the same time with each breath automatically your Awareness Increases. Continue to Increase Awareness through staying with the breath as you receive now the profoundly powerful support of the Sangha of all Dharma's, eager to serve you in Healing, Empowerments, and all that's necessary for full Mastery of Enlightenment. *Allow* any Teachers, Deities, and Wisdom specific to

ॐ

your path to come forth through this Force of the Unity of All.

As you are feeling waves of this new energy and information, breath in deeply allowing yourself to receive the immense gifts this sacred moment of now is holding to offer to your well-being. Breath out old patterns of believing yourself to be separate and without support, releasing programming of a confusing world, then breathing in the Limitless Support and Connection with all the Illumined One's of Infinity.

This Energy of support from the "Sangha of all Dharmas" integrates into all aspects of your Energy Field and Being, and emanates constantly into the world facilitating the blossoming of the shinning intention of a Unified Golden Age of Harmony and Well-Being on Earth. Any energy field that comes into contact with your field which is receptive to this Blessing

ॐ

of all Traditions of Blessings automatically receives the gift of this "Dharma Sangha Attunement" package.

If you feel drawn to you can also receive the "Guru Dharma Sangha Attunement" to connect with the Maha Siddha (Great Perfected Being) who as a manifestation to bring awareness to the message of the "Sangha of All" to Earth, has completed over six years of meditation without food, water, or sleep.

You can connect to this Great Teacher- Guru Dharma Sangha in His all-pervasive state of meditative consciousness from anywhere in order to receive complete teachings, guidance, instruction, and empowerments. Be able to be present, and Aware so that you can listen, He certainly has the Omni-present power to guide, you only have to be able to get in touch within. Although Guru Dharma Sangha maintains the appearance of a

ॐ

physical body here on Earth, this body is probably already nearing the state of a perfected body of light, *if* He has not already perfected the "Rainbow Body of Light," considering He has been engaged in intense non-stop practice without food or water for over six years...

In order to facilitate a "Guru Dharma Sangha Attunement" simply practice what you have learned through this book and just ask for the "download" you intend to receive. Remember your breath, the state of allow, and your immense support.

ॐ

ॐ

Book Ending

You now have an immense bank of support and a good set of tools to facilitate healing for yourself and others through a relationship with Quantum Field Energy. Be inspired to explore and experiment drawing forth even greater wonders of Being from the never ending possibilities offered by the ever present Energy of the Unified Quantum Field.

Trust in your Healing/Guidance Team and the Primordial Limitless Energy. Feel the Love that this infinite field of resources to experience of Being is a product of. Regardless of appearances at any given moment be Grateful for the immense opportunities that Reality as Infinite Possibilities offers.

This Infinite Ocean of the Unified Quantum Field accompanies your every

ॐ

step, in this way your every step is blessed, and everywhere you go is blessed.

Every time you discover the moment of Now is blessed with infinite possibilities. You have always been moving in this boundless Ocean of Energy, all that is and is not comes to be through this Primordial Power.

Welcome to an Empowered multi-dimensional world of Unity and Support. Many welcomes to the Divine play-ground of the Unified Field of Energy-Infinity. Infinite Gratitude for Being Here sharing in this boundless moment of Now.

The Super Conscious Energy of Infinity guides the completion and empowerment of all attunements linked by this book between Quantum Field and reader. These blessings and energies continue to multiply and gather strength always in a safe and comfortable way, as long as they are desired and are of assistance.

ॐ

I hope you enjoyed the reading, and again do feel free to send me an email (darshan@siddha-life-mastery.com) with any questions, comments, experiences, etc. It's great to get these emails, and though sometimes I get a lot of email and can't respond to everything, I do read them, and I try to answer as many as possible!

Want some more pragmatic tools to apply this energy awareness? You may want to check out the new FREE COURSE mentioned below. You get access to some great videos, pdf downloads, and more with powerful tools you can use for Mastery in life!

Gain more practical tools and interaction with the author Darshan Baba! **Go to** http://siddha-life-mastery.com **now to sign up for a free online course**: Introduction and Experience of Subtle Energy, includes Ancient Secret of the Masters – a Simple Breathing Technique for Increased

ॐ

Awareness, Intelligence, Energy, Health, & Personal Power.

FREE Ebook copy of "A Self Attunement: Maha Moksha Healing" Now available at http://siddha-international.weebly.com Follow the link to get instant access to download!

Made in the USA
Coppell, TX
01 May 2021

54817738R00069